THE
BATTLE
of
BUNKER HILL

A HISTORY PERSPECTIVES BOOK

Marcia Amidon Lusted

Published in the United States of America by Cherry Lake Publishing
Ann Arbor, Michigan
www.cherrylakepublishing.com

Consultants: Peter C. Vermilyea, Lecturer, History Department, Western
Connecticut State University; Marla Conn, ReadAbility, Inc.
Editorial direction: Red Line Editorial
Book design and illustration: Sleeping Bear Press

Photo Credits: Felix Octavius Carr Darley/Library of Congress, cover
(left), 1 (left); Percy Moran/Library of Congress, cover (middle), 1
(middle), 20; North Wind Picture Archives/AP Images, cover (right), 1
(right); North Wind Picture Archives, 4, 13, 14, 15, 17, 22, 24, 26, 28, 30;
Library of Congress, 6, 10; Sarony & Major/Library of Congress, 8

Library of Congress Cataloging-in-Publication Data
Lusted, Marcia Amidon.
    The Battle of Bunker Hill / Marcia Amidon Lüsted.
        pages cm. – (Perspectives library)
    ISBN 978-1-62431-414-8 (hardcover) – ISBN 978-1-62431-490-2 (pbk.)
– ISBN 978-1-62431-452-0 (pdf) – ISBN 978-1-62431-528-2 (ebook)
    1. Bunker Hill, Battle of, Boston, Mass., 1775–Juvenile literature. 2.
Massachusetts–History–Revolution, 1775-1783–Juvenile literature. I. Title.
E241.B9L87 2013
973.3'312–dc23
                            2013006361

Cherry Lake Publishing would like to acknowledge the work of
The Partnership for 21st Century Skills. Please visit www.p21.org
for more information.

Printed in the United States of America
Corporate Graphics Inc.
July 2013
CLFA11

TABLE OF CONTENTS

In this book, you will read about the Battle of Bunker Hill from three perspectives. Each perspective is based on real things that happened to real people who were either at Bunker Hill or lived in Boston during the Revolutionary War. As you'll see, the same event can look different depending on one's point of view.

1

Samuel Chase

Minuteman

As we marched toward Boston on that warm morning of June 17, 1775, I could hear the thundering of cannons and the whistling of the cannonballs flying through the air. Yet our commander, Colonel John Stark, marched us four miles at a steady pace. I wanted to run toward Bunker Hill and begin firing at the redcoats. I was a minuteman and ready to lead the

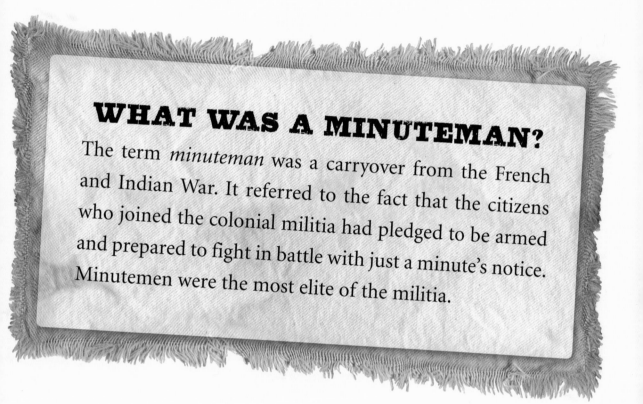

WHAT WAS A MINUTEMAN?

The term *minuteman* was a carryover from the French and Indian War. It referred to the fact that the citizens who joined the colonial militia had pledged to be armed and prepared to fight in battle with just a minute's notice. Minutemen were the most elite of the militia.

charge. But Colonel Stark told us "one fresh man in action is worth ten fatigued men" and refused to increase our pace.

Most of us, 1,200 in all, had never before left the peaceful fields and woods of New Hampshire. But as soon as we heard the news of the first battle with the British at Lexington, Massachusetts, we rushed to the seacoast of New Hampshire. We formed a **regiment**

▲ *The Battles of Lexington and Concord marked the beginning of the Revolutionary War.*

under Colonel Stark. Now we were going to drive the British out of Boston. The British might have more soldiers, but we were fighting for our own country. That made us stronger.

Before the battles at Lexington and Concord in Massachusetts two months ago, it seemed most of us living in the colonies were still trying to find ways to remain loyal British subjects. After all, we were English and proud of it. But recent events had strained our loyalties. **Parliament** kept adding taxes that we were expected to pay. With the Stamp Act, the British taxed all official documents. Many protested this. The situation grew tense, especially in Boston, as patriots—no longer do I think of them as just **radicals**—clashed with British soldiers in March 1770. British soldiers killed five of our colonists on King Street during a skirmish I now hear referred to as the Boston Massacre.

Then the British passed the Tea Act in 1773, which taxed one of our favorite beverages. Samuel Adams of Boston brought together a small group of patriots to protest what they called "taxation without representation." It meant British Parliament should not tax us if we had no say in how we are governed. I was glad to hear of the Boston Tea Party, when a

▲ *Colonists protested against taxation on tea during the Boston Tea Party.*

group of these patriots protested the tax by dumping a shipment of tea from England into Boston Harbor. We were all beginning to feel as if the actions of this group spoke for most of us in the colonies. The British put a stranglehold on Boston Harbor, preventing shipments in or out. Samuel Adams and his secret freedom group, the Sons of Liberty, began working toward a new idea: independence from Britain. Why should we be ruled by a king who clearly did not care about us?

Then, in April 1775, the first shots were fired between patriots and British soldiers at Lexington Green. Conflict was becoming war, and as I marched toward Bunker Hill, I knew that this was the right thing to do. I was going to help fight the British for our freedom.

Under Colonel Stark, we marched just north of Boston across Charlestown Neck, a narrow strip of land linking Charlestown Peninsula with the mainland. Ahead of us was Bunker Hill, where some patriots were already engaged with the British troops. The smell of gunpowder in the air was overwhelming. British warships anchored in Boston Harbor let loose cannonball after cannonball on both hills. Some were

THINK ABOUT IT

▶ Determine the main point of the previous paragraph and pick out one piece of evidence that supports it.

"hotshots," which were cannonballs heated red hot. The British also fired carcasses, which were hollowed-out cannonballs filled with pitch and set on fire. Soon all Charlestown was burning.

▲ At Bunker Hill, patriot troops tried to hold back British soldiers.

Colonel Stark stopped us on the beach of the Mystic River, just east of Bunker Hill. We took shelter behind a low stone wall. General Israel Putnam joined us with some of his Connecticut soldiers. Soon 350 British soldiers advanced down the beach toward us. The sun glinted off their steel **bayonets**, which were drawn and ready. The

SECOND SOURCE

▶ Find another source describing the beginnings of the Battle of Bunker Hill and compare the information there to the information in this source.

sea of red from the soldiers' coats was a terrifying sight. As they charged our wall, I heard General Putnam say, "Don't fire until you see the whites of their eyes!"

Then our first line of **militia** suddenly stood and fired. When they ducked down to reload, the British advanced, and another line of militia stood, fired, and then reloaded. Bullets were dear, so we had to shoot with careful aim and make every bullet count. The air was thick with musket balls and gunpowder. The sun beat down on my head, but I kept reloading and firing, even as sweat dripped down my face. The grass became slick with the blood of redcoats. In all, 96 redcoats were killed.

Our group of soldiers saw the redcoats retreat at Bunker Hill. But, alas, the redcoats were able to break through our lines on Breed's Hill, which was south of us and closer to Boston. Colonel William Prescott, who was commanding our troops there, finally ordered a retreat. But our men made it a fighting retreat. As we moved back across Charlestown Neck to the mainland, more redcoats fell under our musket fire. Many more of our patriots fell here as well. We lost the battle, but we did not feel like losers. We farmers, merchants, and fishermen had delivered a bloody blow to the professional soldiers of His Majesty's British Army.

▲ *The British were able to break through patriot lines on Breed's Hill.*

Simon Lawrence

British Soldier

As our longboat was rowed across the water from Long Wharf in Boston toward Charlestown, I could see the rebels digging on the hills there. I could not shake the feeling that some of those men once could have been my neighbors in Britain. Certainly there were many who had considered themselves to be loyal subjects of King George, just as I did. So how did I come to be here, in this colonial city, ready to fight them? What had happened?

Negative attitudes against British rule had been growing in the American colonies. A couple years ago, in 1770, our own British soldiers accidentally fired shots, killing five colonists. What the colonials began calling the Boston Massacre was the first moment of bloodshed between us. It worsened our relations greatly and made us look like the enemy.

I had been sent to Boston a year ago, in 1774. As our British ships blocked Boston Harbor, there was a

◄ Colonists protested against taxes, such as the Stamp Act, that Parliament imposed on them.

need for more of His Majesty's soldiers to keep the peace. At first it was not so bad. Many of these rebels were still loyal to England, and we seemed to be able to live together. But Parliament **levied** more taxes on the colonies, and rightly so. It was trying to pay back the costs of the war with the French and the Indians, when we helped to protect these colonies. Yet with each new tax, it seemed that these colonials became resentful. They were outraged that they did not have someone from the colonies to represent them in Parliament. Soon our troops faced some of their so-called minutemen in Lexington and Concord. Suddenly it had become a war, a war that as a loyal British subject, I did not understand.

Our ships were blasting the hills of Charlestown with cannonballs as we stepped off our boat and onto

ANALYZE THIS

▶ Analyze another account of British taxation in this book and compare it to this one. How are they different?

British soldiers marched toward Bunker and Breed's Hills to engage the Americans.

the peninsula on June 17, 1775. General William Howe, our commander, gave orders that we should march around the back of the American forces and attack. As we moved into position, though, I could see that there were many more rebels on Bunker Hill and Breed's Hill than we had expected. They had dug themselves in with trenches and walls for protection.

General Howe ordered us to halt and wait for reinforcements. Then he ordered several hundred of us to take positions along the beach. There we saw a

BUNKER HILL AND BREED'S HILL

The famous Revolutionary War battle of June 1775 is known as the Battle of Bunker Hill. But it isn't an accurate name since much more fighting took place on Breed's Hill. Breed's Hill was lower than Bunker Hill, but it was located in the middle of Charlestown peninsula and closer to Boston. Bunker Hill was located on the northern shore of Charlestown.

group of rebels sheltered behind a stone wall. General Howe formed us into a line and we marched forward. I had my bayonet out and was ready to strike, but I was frightened by the ferocious fighting going on all around me. These rebels should have been no match for us. We were professionally trained soldiers, and I was in General Howe's finest light **infantry**.

We drew closer and closer to the rebels. They did not fight by any of the rules of battle that I had learned. Suddenly they stood up in a line and fired at us. Musket balls flew through the air, and I felt a tug on my shoulder and realized I had been hit. I continued to move towards their lines. Surely the time it would take them to reload their clumsy muskets would be enough time for us to strike. But then another line of rebels stood and fired. This time I felt a bullet graze my leg, and I fell. My friend, James, soon fell as well, his blood soaking into the grass. As I lay there, I could see more of my company fall around me under the relentless musket fire of these rebels. Perhaps we had failed to understand. They were not rebels. They were patriots. And a man who is fighting for his freedom and independence is

SECOND SOURCE

▶ Find another source describing the British advance toward Bunker Hill and compare the information there to the information in this source.

much stronger than a man who is fighting on the orders of his king and his commanders.

The pounding of cannonballs and the noise of gunfire swirled around me. More and more British soldiers fell. Soon I heard General Howe give the order to fall back. Fall back! Retreat from these farmers? I tried to get up but could not, so I watched as the

▲ *British troops tried to gain ground at Bunker Hill.*

remaining men in my company joined forces with General Robert Pigot. His men had been attacking the top of Breed's Hill. Again, I watched in disbelief as the rebels fought off our soldiers. They fought until it seemed they ran out of ammunition. Soon our redcoats swept up and over the hill to win the battle.

My fellow British soldiers took me to a house in Boston where other wounded British soldiers were being cared for. There I heard we had finally won the battle. But it was with a high cost. Hundreds of us were wounded and around 200 were dead. I heard later that the cost of the war to us was almost greater than the benefits. I could not escape the thought that the men of this new America, men who had managed to stand against us, were men who once shared my loyalty to king and country. I was just beginning to understand that this was not simply a **rebellion** to be put down so that King George's rule would continue. It was something much greater than that.

3

Molly Whittaker

Innkeeper

My husband and I have run the Green Dragon Tavern since 1765, for well on ten years now. It's a fanciful name for a plain tavern in Boston, I know, but I like it. For years now, we've been a gathering place for Boston folks and British soldiers alike.

But times have changed, I can tell you. Once there was friendliness between us all. Boston men would share drinks with British officers. They traded stories about life in England and life here. We still felt like we were connected, all of us subjects of King George. But since that nasty business with the Boston Massacre back in 1770, with five of our own dead because of the British, tempers are quick to flare.

THE BOSTON MASSACRE

The Boston Massacre took place on March 5, 1770. It started when a crowd of American colonists began yelling and jeering at a British soldier. A group of other British soldiers came to support the soldier against the crowd. The colonists continued to yell and throw snowballs. Finally the British soldiers fired at them. Five Americans were killed. Later the British officer in charge and eight of his men were arrested for manslaughter, but they were not convicted.

Not many British officers dare to show their faces in the Green Dragon anymore. And there's been many a time when I knew that plans were being hatched in this very tavern, at my own tables in the back corner. In fact, it wouldn't surprise me to find that some of Samuel Adams's secret Sons of Liberty group had planned their tea party over tankards of our ale.

▲ *The Sons of Liberty met to discuss ways to protest Parliament's taxation.*

We got a chuckle over that one, you can count on it. Imagine patriots, dressed like Indians, emptying crates of tea into Boston Harbor! Now we drink coffee. I miss my cup of tea, but I will not put up with another tax put upon us by the king.

I'm no rebel. I was born and bred in England, and I was once proud to call myself British. I was just as happy to tease and joke with the redcoats as anyone. Some of them reminded me of boys I once knew back in London. But things change, first with the massacre, and then with this business of battles and bloodshed at Lexington and Concord. The British have put Boston under **siege**. There is not enough food, and we have been forced to **quarter** even more British officers and soldiers in our public houses.

ANALYZE THIS

▶ Analyze another account of the Boston Tea Party in this book and compare it to this one. How are they alike? How are they different?

We are patriots and Americans now. It feels like war has come, and even more so as of last week. A true battle it was, but this time closer to home. Our patriots fought the redcoats at Bunker and Breed's Hills, just across the Charles River at Charlestown.

During the day of the battle, the thumping of British cannon fire from their warships was enough to make me want to cower in the cellar. It felt like the very foundations of the tavern would collapse. A cloud of gunpowder seemed to hang over the city in the hot, still June air. Soon the wounded

◀ *The battle was heard by colonists in Boston.*

started to be brought back to the city. I cleared out rooms upstairs for nursing them. Many Boston women opened their homes for the wounded as well. Far too many died from the wounds they were given by British guns and bayonets.

Now the siege continues. My husband has joined General George Washington's patriot force in Cambridge. It is no longer safe for him to venture here, where there are so many British soldiers. We are all hungry here in the city. I've even heard of people eating rats! Our consolation is that the British are hungry too. They might control Boston Harbor and the ships that can come and go, but they also await their own supply ships.

Still, the British take whatever they want from our homes, including the food from our mouths. I notice that they do not bother to find out if they are stealing from a patriot or one of their own **loyalists**. There is precious little ale and even less food to serve

▲ *British troops took food and supplies from colonists' homes.*

in the tavern. Business has fallen off, and no plans are being made over my tables anymore. The tavern and my family are forced to rely on salted cod and other foods I preserved and hid in the attic. But they will not last us much longer. Beans, pork, and fish (when my son can catch it) are all we eat, as fresh meat is too scarce and costly. Even wood for the fire is difficult to come by and expensive.

I fear for my children, as we are frequently under fire from both patriots and British, fighting each other. But I know that we can withstand this siege, and the war that has come, if it means our freedom from the tyranny of Britain and King George. My children are Americans, born and bred here in Boston. And even though my husband and I came here from England, we are also Americans. As I bathed the faces of those brave men who fought the redcoats on Bunker Hill and tried to bind their wounds, I knew that revolution had come to us. And I know that I have no regrets, no matter what losses I face.

THINK ABOUT IT

▶ Determine the main point of this chapter and pick out one piece of evidence that supports it.

LOOK, LOOK AGAIN

This is an artist's version of the fighting on Breed's Hill. Study the illustration and answer the following questions:

1. Imagine you are a minuteman. What would you think when you saw the British advancing?

2. Imagine you are a British soldier. How would you describe this scene in a letter to your family?

3. Imagine you are an innkeeper in Boston. What would you think if you saw this scene from the battle?

GLOSSARY

bayonet (BAY-uh-net) a blade attached to a rifle that can be used as a weapon

infantry (IN-fuhn-tree) soldiers who march or fight on foot instead of on horseback

levy (LEV-ee) to collect by lawful means or by force

loyalist (LOI-uh-list) a colonist who supported the British during the Revolutionary War

parliament (PAHR-luh-muhnt) a group of people who make or change laws in a country or state, such as the United Kingdom

quarter (KWOR-tur) to house in a dwelling

radical (RAD-i-kuhl) a person working for political or social change

rebellion (ri-BEL-yuhn) the process of resisting a government or ruler, often violently

regiment (REJ-uh-muhnt) a military unit made up of two or more battalions

siege (SEEJ) surrounding a place to cut it off from supplies in an attempt to force those inside to surrender

LEARN MORE

Further Reading

Catel, Patrick. *Battles of the Revolutionary War.* Chicago: Heinemann Library, 2011.
Murray, Stuart. *American Revolution.* New York: DK, 2005.
Perritano, John. *The Causes of the American Revolution.* New York: Crabtree, 2013.

Web Sites

Battle of Bunker Hill
http://www.history.com/topics/battle-of-bunker-hill
This Web site has information and videos about Bunker Hill and the American Revolution.

The Battle of Bunker Hill
http://www.masshist.org/revolution/bunkerhill.php
This Web site has more information about the battle, as well as articles and letters from the time period.

INDEX

ABOUT THE AUTHOR

Marcia Amidon Lusted is the author of 75 books and 350 magazine articles for young readers. She grew up in New England and has visited many American Revolution historic sites, including the Bunker Hill Monument in Charlestown, Massachusetts.